Why do so many bad things happen?

CHINE McDONALD

He will wipe every tear from their eyes. There will be no more death or mourning or crying or pain, for the old order of things has passed away.

From the Bible: Revelation chapter 21 verse 4

Contents

Everybody asks...

Most people will at some point in their lives experience suffering: from the loss of a job or the breakdown of a relationship, to tragic circumstances, including illness and bereavement. These are things that are experienced by people all over the world from the richest countries to the poorest. Coming to terms with the fact that bad things happen seems to be part of the human experience.

On top of bad things happening to individuals, we see how bad things happen on a global scale - economic, racial and gender injustices, natural disasters and humanitarian emergencies, famine and genocide.

Sometimes the sheer scale and frequency of these horrors can feel overwhelming. So much suffering, so much pain.

It is no wonder that we find ourselves asking: why do so many bad things happen?

The question usually comes when we personally experience pain and suffering, or we witness others going through difficult times, whether those people are close to us or far away. Something in us asks the question: why?

Why do floods, droughts and storms happen, causing death and destruction among some of the world's poorest and most marginalised communities?

Why do children suffer from terminal illnesses?

Why do some in our country live in abject poverty, while others have more wealth than they could spend in a lifetime?

Why do racism, sexism and all other forms of prejudice exist, causing division and harm to many?

Why do so many people suffer from mental illness?

Why do senseless accidents happen that cut lives short and deprive families of their l oved ones?

If there is a God who is supposed to be good, then why does God allow these bad things to happen?

Christians believe...

...that God is good.

God is the essence of goodness and that all goodness has God at its source.

Christians also believe that God created the world and called it 'good' – and not just the world, but the universe and all that exists. Moreover, God created humans so God and humanity can exist in relationship with each other.

But Christians also know that evil exists in the world; that terrible things take place.

Just like everyone else, Christians have to face the question: how could a good God create a world in which bad things happen? All of us have to face the puzzling contradiction of how the world can be both awe-inspiring – and also a place where catastrophes can strike in the form of natural disasters. The world is stunningly beautiful, yet also flawed.

Christian thinkers throughout the centuries have tried to answer this question. The problem of evil is a difficult thing to reconcile with belief in a good and loving God.

For some people the existence of evil is in itself enough evidence that God does not exist. But for Christians, God's goodness is not in doubt, despite the existence of evil.

Although evil remains a problem and can never be described as good, there are different ideas that help Christians reconcile the existence of God with the fact that bad things happen.

When bad things happen, there are a number of different reactions that Christians might have; different ways they might reconcile these happenings with a God of love.

Some accept suffering because they believe ultimately in a sense of divine purpose; that God has a long view of individual and human history and that at some point in the future - in a life that is yet to come - the bad things will make sense and that we will be able to see that ultimately it led to some good.

It's as if we are watching a game of chess and God is the grandmaster. We have no idea what his gameplan is - all we can see is the next square.

When it comes to suffering caused by humans, Christians believe that God has given each of us free will. We are free to make our own decisions, to direct our own paths. Free to do good. But this also means we are free to do bad things, too.

It's easier to explain these bad things that happen as a result of human actions. People murder, steal, lie and cheat as a result of being free to choose to do things that hurt others, or themselves.

We see this in the way that children behave. They sometimes do things that are wrong, causing pain to themselves or to others. While good parents want to keep their children from causing harm, they know that their children have to be free to make those choices.

Some Christians over the centuries have explained that bad things happen because in creating the world, God designed it to have the possibility of evil within it, despite being created good.

Christians are hopeful people. Despite all the bad things that we see around the world and in our personal lives and in those of the people we love, hope is something we cling to.

This hope doesn't make us pretend that positive thinking will make everything OK and protect us from the bad things that happen. Anyone who watches the news sees that it would be foolish to think that Christianity is some sort of shield that means only good things will come our way.

Instead, this hope is an eternal one. It's a hope that says although there are so many bad things happening around me, and in the world at large, ultimately things will be made right by God in the end.

In a strange way, the question: 'why do so many bad things happen' points to the existence of God. Perhaps we feel a sense of anger and injustice at these things happening because something within us recognises these bad things as bad.

Christians believe in an ultimate source of morality - God. We have this instinctive sense of things being unfair, unjust, wrong or just bad, because we have something within us linking us to God and to a sense of what good is and therefore how a good world should be.

God whispers to us in our pleasures, speaks in our conscience, but shouts in our pains: it is his megaphone to rouse a deaf world.

CS Lewis, 1898–1963, writer and academic, in 'The Problem of Pain'

The Bible is the basic book that guides Christian belief. It is a collection of writing in different styles, by different authors - poetry, history, letters and more - gathered between 2,000 and 3,000 years ago.

This Bible describes God as:

Eternal
God has no beginning and no end. God existed before anything else existed, spanning through history and billions of years. God has no beginning and no end.

Everywhere
God does not stand separate to creation but exists everywhere in it.

All-powerful
God is able to do all things. Although evil exists in the world, there is nothing more powerful than God and ultimately God will make all things new, bringing about justice and peace that lasts for all eternity.

All-knowing
God hears every thought and listens to every word when we pray. God knows the beginning from the end, and nothing is a surprise to God.

Good

Even when we might doubt God when we see bad things happen, God's intentions are always good. God is the ultimate expression of goodness.

Holy

God is utterly perfect. Nothing can match God's purity. But God also loves us with a breath-taking kind of love.

Above gender

However you try to describe God, God is bigger and greater. This includes using the words 'he' and 'she'. This booklet has tried to steer clear of male pronouns for God, as much as possible, because any sense of God being male or female falls short of reality.

One

Although we can encounter God in different ways as the creator God, Jesus Christ in human form and the Spirit of God alive and active in the world, they are all one and the same. Sometimes Christians refer to God as Father, Son and Holy Spirit. But still, God is one, just as H_2O is ice, water and steam – taking different forms but remaining the same.

Part of what makes it so difficult for people to reconcile the existence of a good God with the existence of evil is that some people do not like the idea of a distant God sitting back and doing nothing while people suffer.

If God is good, then surely God should do something about all the bad things that are happening all over the world.

But one of the most beautiful Christian beliefs is that God doesn't sit back at all.

At the start of the first century, something wonderful happened. In a great big cosmic act of love, God became a vulnerable human being. No longer distant, God bridged the gap between God and humanity by becoming the person we know as Jesus Christ, the founder of Christianity.

For God so loved the world that he gave his one and only Son, that whoever believes in him shall not perish but have eternal life.

From the Bible, describing Jesus: John chapter 3 verse 16

Jesus was born into a humble family, arriving into the world without the pomp and ceremony that you might expect to accompany the arrival of the creator of the universe.

Most historians agree, he was born into a Jewish family, just over 2,000 years ago, in a place in the Middle East now shared by Israel and Palestine.

Raised in the Jewish faith, he began his preaching and teaching when he was 30 years old. His message was something new, however. He spoke about God's love for all of humanity. A love that disregarded all the rules that people had created as ways to get close to God. He spoke of a love that set people free.

This liberation was something that many of his fellow Jewish people longed for. They had been brutally ruled by the Roman Empire for a long time. People were drawn to Jesus, including around a dozen men from different backgrounds, who became his followers.

Jesus and these followers – his disciples – travelled from town to town, gathering crowds. Everyone wanted to see this Jesus, who became known for the healing and other miracles he performed, which pointed the way to God.

The number of his followers grew and grew; men and women wanted to know more about Jesus, and about God.

Jesus's message was one of hope, peace, freedom and love. Just the kinds of things that people wanted to hear. But Jesus also said things that made people uncomfortable. He spoke about a radical kind of love, even love for our enemies.

Jesus spoke about the need for forgiveness – forgiveness for what we have all done wrong, and forgiveness for those who have wronged us.

This message – although hard at times, especially in the face of all the bad things happening – was one of hope. It spoke about a different kind of kingdom, the kingdom of God, in which all of the brokenness in this world would be made whole.

Jesus's preaching and teaching went on for three years. He spent that time travelling, making friends with people from all walks of life, and speaking to them about his message of hope.

The historic accounts that we read in the Bible tell us about Jesus's encounters with people who were often excluded from the rest of society. Those who experienced unimaginable suffering – bereavement, disease, exclusion and loneliness, mental illness, and pain that had lasted for years.

Jesus had compassion for those who he saw experiencing suffering, no matter what their background.

He was openly critical of hypocritical religious leaders, or those who he felt were not demonstrating the love of God.

This criticism was brave. Unsurprisingly the religious leaders were not happy about being called out, and were afraid of Jesus's popularity. Political leaders also feared Jesus's criticism of them to his ever-growing crowds of followers.

Jesus knew that he would suffer at the hands of the authorities, and at various points warned his followers that he would be killed.

For Jesus, this wasn't just a natural consequence of a revolutionary life that rattled those in charge, but part of God's plan.

He spoke about his suffering and death as part of God's plan to save the whole world; to bridge the gap between God and humanity.

Jesus's final few days saw him and his followers arriving in Jerusalem where they were met with crowds of people welcoming them. Many of them believed that Jesus's arrival would lead to them being rescued from Roman rule. But the authorities were watching and looking for ways to quash this threat to their power.

On the night before Jesus died, he and his followers ate a meal – their Last Supper together. During the meal, Jesus broke apart a loaf of bread and said it symbolised his body that would be broken. He poured out wine and compared it to his blood that would be shed. Jesus asked his followers to eat the bread and drink the wine to remember him when he was gone.

In churches across the world, Christians regularly eat bread and drink wine as a way to remember Jesus and the meaning of his death.

After the meal, Jesus spent some time praying in a beautiful olive grove. There he wrestled mentally with the suffering he knew he was about to go through. Jesus, heartbroken, argued with God and begged for a way out. But in the end, he said he would do what God wanted, knowing that it would mean that others would not face separation from God.

After he finished praying, Jesus was arrested. One of his followers had collaborated with the authorities and betrayed Jesus. Although Jesus had warned his followers about what was going to happen, they fled.

Jesus was tortured through the night. The next day he stood trial and was accused of blasphemy. It was decided that he would pay the ultimate price - death.

It was not just a quick and painless death. After being paraded through the streets in shame, he had nails hammered through his wrists and ankles to hang him on a wooden cross. This brutal and tortuous execution was known as crucifixion.

While hanging on the cross, Jesus asked God to forgive those who persecuted and killed him.

Jesus's friends and family were devastated by his death. So were the many people who had expected he would save them from Roman rule.

Jesus's body was put in a tomb with a heavy stone laid across the entrance. It seemed that all was lost until God raised Jesus from the dead. Suffering and death turned into hope and life.

On the third day after his death – a Sunday morning – a group of women who had been Jesus's friends and followers went to the tomb and discovered that Jesus was not dead but alive. They ran to tell the disciples. When they visited the tomb to check out the women's story, they found it to be true. He was alive.

The risen Jesus visited his friends several times over the next few weeks. The final time, he asked them to go on telling his story around the world, inviting others to become followers of Jesus for themselves. He promised them that, although he would no longer be with them physically, he would be with them through the Holy Spirit.

Believe, when you are most unhappy, that
there is something for you to do in the world.
So long as you can sweeten another's pain, life is not in vain.

Helen Keller, author, disability rights advocate, political activist

Christians believe that the Holy Spirit is always with them, as if Jesus himself was walking alongside them.

At times of deep suffering, the Holy Spirit Is able to bring God's comfort. When bad things happen, God is right there in the midst of our pain.

God is able to understand our suffering because Jesus suffered the most unimaginable physical and emotional pain. On the cross he felt abandoned by his heavenly father and by his closest friends. He endured separation from God so that we need never be separated from God's love.

This does not mean that we will live lives without suffering. The heartbreaking reality is that bad things will continue to happen. But as most of us know, suffering is made just that little bit more bearable when we are not left alone in it.

The beauty of the Christian story is that God holds our hand through the pain, and that ultimately - through Jesus bridging the gap between God and humanity - we will be united with him in a place where bad things will never happen again.

Blessed are those who mourn, for they will be comforted.

From the Bible: Jesus's life story as told by Matthew chapter 5 verse 4

You could...

Life is full of hard and difficult things. We just have to turn on our TV screens to see that bad things happen in our world; global pandemics that kill millions, natural disasters, terrorist attacks and more. The world can sometimes feel like a dark and scary place.

But on a more individual scale, each of us experiences dark days whether through bereavement, depression or the breakdown of relationships. It's good to talk about these things.

It can be easy to bottle up this sense of fear about the bad things in the world that happen. But you could try talking to God about the fear, anxiety or pain that you feel or are going through, or the pain that others are experiencing.

You could try praying for those you know who are suffering, as well as those who you don't know, including those in some of the poorest and most marginalised communities in the world for whom suffering is a daily reality.

Try talking to God about all of these bad things. God is the only one who can give us eternal hope despite what we see around us.

What can you do when you feel helpless about all the bad things happening?

Have a go at praying.
See what happens.

Find a quiet place. Tell God what is on your mind. Speak about the suffering that you see in your own life, in the lives of those around you, and in the lives of those whose suffering you only hear about on TV news bulletins. Tell God your hopes for making things better. Then say 'Amen' like Christians have for centuries (it means 'yes indeed').

Read a bit of the Bible.

A good place to begin is reading about the life of Jesus and how he helped those in great need. Look for a section called the Gospel of Luke. (It means 'the good news as Luke tells it'.) Find out what Jesus's story tells us about suffering and pain, but also hope and life.

Drop into a church.

Find out what going to a church could offer you. Look at a church's website, phone them up, or ask around and you will get a sense of what kind of events are on offer – whether they are very quiet, particularly family-oriented, contain lots of modern songs, or are more traditional. Perhaps try more than one and see which you find most helpful.

Join a discussion group that weighs up Christian claims.

Many churches have these, with names like the Alpha course, Christianity Explored, or Pilgrim. Go prepared to listen but join in honestly.

Have another go at praying.

Prayer doesn't have to be out loud. Prayer and communication with God can come through silence. God knows what we are going through; the pain that we might be experiencing. Make yourself open to see what God might be saying: how God might be comforting you or others, sometimes in unexpected ways.

Try living with the same values and actions that Jesus had.

Shut your eyes. Take a deep breath. Tell Jesus you'll give following him a go.

Who shall separate us from the love of Christ? Shall trouble or hardship or persecution or famine or nakedness or danger or sword?

From the Bible: Romans chapter 8 verse 35

Explore more...

The website **explorechristianity.info** is a portal that can lead you to much more information. It will help you find answers from a Christian point of view to life's biggest questions.

You will find:

- Information about the Christian faith and its founder Jesus Christ

- Suggestions on how to begin living as a Christian

- Ideas to help faith grow

- Advice about meeting other Christians in churches and cathedrals

- Links to reliable websites where you can discover more.

explorechristianity.info

Notes